MAKING INDIA FRIENDLY FOR THE DIFFERENTLY ABLED

BIPIN MENON

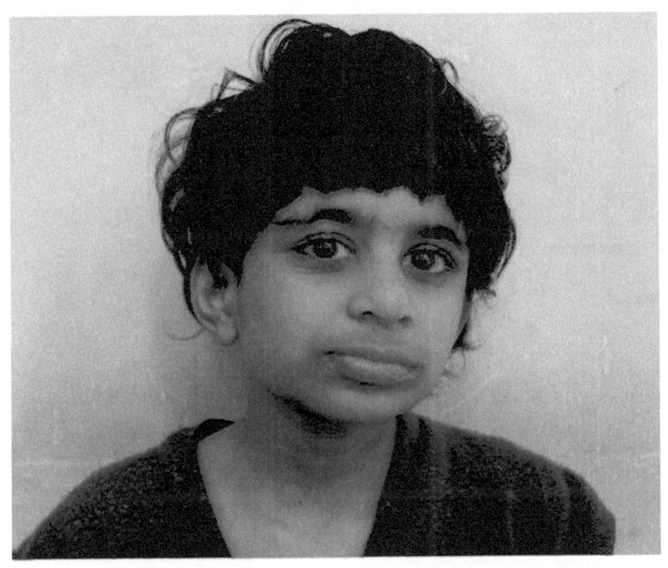

Enter Caption

This book is dedicated to my specially abled daughter Candy (Shruyaani Menon) who has taught us all the virtues of remaining optimistic and positive in life despite all the travails and tribulations .

Contents

Acknowledgements   *vii*

1. Introduction   1
2. Government Initiatives On Accessibility   7
3. Punarbhava And Indian Legal Framework   11
4. National Trust   16
5. Rehabilitation Council Of India   24
6. National Handicapped Finance And Development Corporation (nhfdc)   29
7. Global Celebrities With Disabilities   33
8. Indian Celebrities With Disabilities   41
9. Transport Accessibility - Reality In India   45
10. Personal Experience   51
11. Swiss Experience   58
12. Phelan Mcdermid Syndrome (pms)   61
13. Paralympics   67
14. Ergonomics For Specially Abled Working Space   74
15. Skilling Of People With Disabilities   80
16. Corporate Social Responsibility   87
17. What India Needs?   95
18. Conclusions   100

Acknowledgements

I would like to acknowledge the efforts of my wife Dr Ipseeta Menon and elder daughter Shivangi Menon who motivated me to pen this and helped me throughout with their valuable inputs.

CHAPTER ONE

Introduction

We are all a product of biological processes that apart from being enigmatic are quite complex. The breakdown in this genetic system accentuated by both internal and external factors has led to instances where some humans do not have the same physiological and mental control over their faculties and activities.

Generally referred to as *"specially-abled persons"*, they begin their life with a big barrier, not so much from their own disability, but from the attitude of many so called *able bodied* people around them. As Robert. M. Hensel, who was born with a birth defect called Spina bifida said, *"There is no greater disability in society, than the inability to see a person as more"*

There are many categorizations of the disabilities that afflict persons. These could be intellectual, physical, sensory and mental illness. The World Health Organisation (WHO) has a three tier classification of impairment in the person's body structure or body function or mental functioning. Some other categories of impairments include visual impairment, hearing impairment, motor impairment and cognitive impairment. India's Person with Disabilities (PwD) Act, 1995, disability has been defined as including blindness, low vision, leprosy cured, hearing impairment, locomotor disability, mental retardation and mental illness. Each of these specific classifications of disability requires a different plan of policy action.

The tennis star Martina Navratilova said *"Disability is a matter of perception. If you can do just one thing well, you are needed by someone."* It's akin to the weaknesses of any able bodied sportsperson. Coaches always advise them to focus on their strengths and not allow the weakness to pull them down. It is the very same situation of the specially abled persons who need the right motivation and focus to over compensate their disability and provide them confidence to lead a normal life. There is a hypothesis that on account of their condition, they are able to focus and their other faculty does develop more than even the able bodied.

The performance of the Korean Olympic archer Im Dong-Hyun is a unique case. He had severe myopia and was considered legally blind. He however, had a keen sense of the target and shot a world record in the preliminary rounds of the 2012 London Olympics. He also won the gold as part of the Korean team in the 2004 and 2008 Olympics. However, the ironic aspect was that he refused surgery for correction of his condition since he believed that it provided him with better focus and co-ordination in this demanding sport.

The manifestations of disability are in many forms, both physical and mental. However, despite these disabilities, many are able to refocus their other normal functions to integrate into mainstream society. However, it is important that they get the necessary encouragement from their social milieu as they try to live a normal life. More than sympathy, it is the attitudinal changes that are necessary to accept these people with their inherent disabilities and going that step further to make them feel a part of the social set up. Moreover, there is no *"one size fit all"* approach as each case has its specificities. Very difficult to pen down but it's probably about the right balance between trying to help at each step to making them feel independent to undertake their activities. It is imperative that they are provided optimism and confidence to overcome the societal pressures. As Helen Keller said *"Optimism is the faith that leads to achievement. Nothing can be done without hope and confidence."*

The key aspect for any policies related to this arena is to identifying the cases at the nascent stage and then giving the best possible medical care for preventing any deterioration or even working on the affected faculties. The next stage then has to be about rehabilitation and empowering them to undertake some vocational course that would enable them to the gainfully employed. This financial independence is the crux of the inclusivity and assimilation of the specially abled people into society. Moreover, some of the organisations and agencies who have a structured plan for recruitment of specially abled people even vouch that in certain vocations, they perform better than the abled bodied persons primarily on account of their focus and sharper development of other faculties.

It is also important to have a strong regulatory framework to ensure that the specially abled have adequate rights to ensure legal protection and fair treatment without discrimination.

The gravity of this problem can be better understood from the 2011 census of India which put the number of people with disabilities at 26.8 million. However, some other studies indicate that that it could be higher. Globally, the WHO in its report estimates that nearly 15% of global population, accounting for around a billion people suffer from some form of disability or the other. It is important for governments to understand that with the right policies and attitudinal change, they can actually be assets in the economic development of any nation, a far cry from the general perception that they could be a burden on resources. Finally, as the blind Chinese activist Chen Guangcheng said *"how a society treats its disabled is a true measure of its civilization"*.

The book focuses specifically from the perspective of a developing country like India. While dwelling on the regulatory framework and the plethora of policies and schemes available for the specially abled, it also provides a snapshot of famous celebrities who had some disabilities but managed to carve a niche in their field. There is a section on the exhilarating performance of the specially abled athletes in the Paralympics and how the Games have provided a completely new perspective on their abilities. It also talks about how the corporates need to come forward with targeted policies for ensuring sustainable skilling and inclusivity of the specially abled persons.

Moreover, it seeks to understand what these specially-abled persons have to go though, especially when living in societies where attitudes can sway from complete ignorance to even disdain. As they say *"the only disability in life is a bad attitude."* It does not seek to criticize anyone but aims to foster an environment which is empathetic to these specially-abled men, women and children as they struggle with the challenges thrown at by life.

Government Initiatives on Accessibility

The Government of India has a structured policy on people with disabilities. These policies are formulated through the Department of Empowerment of People with Disabilities (DEPwD) also known as Divyangjan. This Department is under the Ministry of Social Justice and Empowerment.

The vision of this department is to build an inclusive society in which equal opportunities are provided for the growth and development of Persons with Disabilities so that they can lead productive, safe and dignified lives. On the other hand, its mission is to empower Persons with Disabilities, through its various Acts/ Institutions/Organizations and Schemes for rehabilitation and to create an enabling environment that provide such persons with equal opportunities, protection of their rights and enable them to participate as independent and productive members of society. It is however only by this empowerment through specific interventions that the vision of an inclusive society can be achieved.

One of the flagship programmes of DEPwD is the *"Accessible India Campaign"* or the *"Sugamya Bharat Abhiyan"*. This is structured around three key objectives namely creating an accessible environment in government buildings; improving and creating accessible public transport systems; and accessibility to information and communication such as public documents and creation of pool of sign language interpreters.

The first objective of making government buildings disabled friendly has been ensconced through specific targets set. The actual work involves having requisite steps, ramps, corridors, entry gates, emergency exits and parking. The indoor and outdoor facilities including lighting, signages, alarm systems and toilets are also supposed to be tailored to be disabled friendly. An annual accessibility audit in line with international standards such as ISO 21542:2011 relating to construction, assembly, components and fittings is crucial. The first of these targets is to conduct accessibility audit of atleast 25-50 important government buildings and converting them into accessible buildings in select 50 cities. Subsequently, 50% of the government buildings in the national capitals and state capitals are to be made disabled friendly. The final target is to conduct audit and convert 50% of the buildings as accessible friendly in ten major towns of all states.

The second objective is to make the transportation system accessible to the disabled. These systems would cover air, rail and bus travel. In the case of the airport, two targets were set, firstly to convert all international airports into disabled friendly and then convert all the domestic airports too. On rail travel, the first target is for all A1, A and B railway stations to be disabled friendly. Subsequently, 50% of all the other railway stations are to be made disabled friendly. The most challenging aspect is of course the road public transport. In this case the target is to convert 25% of all public transport carriers into being disabled friendly.

The final objective is to make the information and communication eco-system disabled accessible. This includes the public documents, websites, creation of talent pool of sign language interpreters and making television programmes accessible. The targets set in this include conducting accessibility audits of 50% of all central and state government websites and providing accessibility to 50% of all public documents as per the ISO/IEC 40500:2012, IT-W3C web content accessibility guidelines (WCAG) 2.0. The next target is to create an additional pool of 200 sign language interpreters who meet the professional standards. In terms of television, the twin targets are firstly to create standards for captioning and sign language interpretation for public television news programs and then ensuring that 25% of all programs meet these standards.

The entire accessible India campaign seeks to ensure that an enabling environment is created for the disabled to effectively utilize the public services meant for them. The private sector has also been encouraged to adopt these practices through their CSR funds.

However, while one pillar of this entire campaign is focussed on the creation of the infrastructure and enabling environment by the government and private agencies, the more arduous task is to create the requisite mindset among the abled body members of society. Ultimately, it is those attitudes and maintenance of the infrastructure created that would determine the success of the campaign.

CHAPTER THREE

Punarbhava and Indian Legal Framework

Punarbhava, literally translated into re-becoming or re-born is closely associated with the concept of re-birth. The name has been aptly chosen for a national interactive web portal on disability. The underlying aim is to provide a fresh lease of life to people with disabilities so that they could lead a normal life.

The website is intended to be a one stop shop for people with disabilities and their guardians. The aim is to provide a snapshot of the regulatory framework, list of institutions working in the area, list of schemes available for people with disabilities, resources available etc.

The key regulations for specially abled persons in India are the Mental Health Act 1987, Rehabilitation Council of India (RCI) Act 1992, Persons with Disabilities (PwD) Act 1995 and National Trust Act

1999. Subsequently, the Right of Persons with Disabilities Act was promulgated in 2016. However, some of the other legislations that have some provisions relating to specially abled persons are The Workmen's Compensation Act 1923, Right to Information Act 2005, National Rural Employment Guarantee Assurance (NREGA) Act and Right to Education Act.

The Mental Health Act looks at provisions for the treatment and care of mentally ill persons including the management of their assets. The Act is administered by the Ministry of Health and Family Welfare and deals with persons requiring treatment for mental disorders, as against those with mental retardation. There are institutional mechanisms created at the Central and State level for the administration of the provisions. These are the Central Mental Health Authority and State Mental Health Authorities for which rules were framed in 1990.

The RCI Act deals with the administration of training programmes for the specially abled people. The PwD Act dwells on the full participation and equality of people with disabilities. The National Trust Act relates to the Constitution of the National Trust which runs a number of programmes related for those with autism, celebral palsy, mental retardation and multiple disabilities.

The Persons with Disabilities (Equal Opportunities, Protection of Rights and Full Participation) Act, 1995 was a precursor to the later legislation of 2016 for people with disabilities. It looks at the institutional mechanism such as Central Coordination Committee, State Coordination Committees, Chief Commissioner and Commissioners for Disabilities; education; employment; affirmative action; non-discrimination; research and manpower development; and social security.

The National Trust Act, 1999 is the legislative framework that created the National Trust. This is a key organization that runs several schemes for welfare of people with disabilities. It categorises the target section into those with autism, celebral palsy, mental retardation and multiple disabilities. The Schemes administered by trust are elucidated in subsequent chapters.

The Right of Persons with Disabilities Act, 2016 is an all-encompassing legislation that provides equality of opportunity, rights and protection for people with disabilities. Some of the key aspects of this Act are the enforcement of the key aspects and principles of equality, non-discrimination, protection, safety, reproductive rights, family and guardianship, access to voting, justice, education, skilling, employment, social security, health, rehabilitation, recreation and sporting activities. It places responsibility on the government to ensure access to transportation, information and communication technology, consumer goods etc for those with disabilities. It has provisions for registration of institutions working for disabled and the issuance of certificate of disability. The Act provides an institutional mechanism, human resources, and financial resources for undertaking work for those with disabilities such as the Central Advisory Board on Disability, State Advisory Boards on Disability, Chief Commissioners and State Commissioners for persons with disability, Special Courts, National Fund for People with Disabilities, State Fund for People with Disabilities etc. The Rules for the implementation of the provisions were framed in 2017.

The institutions that are working on specific activities related to the disabled are Ali Yavar Jung National Institute of Speech and Hearing Disabilities (AYJNISHD), Mumbai; National Institute for the Empowerment of People with Intellectual Disabilities (NIEPID), Secunderabad; National Institute for Locomotor Disabilities (NILD), Kolkata; National Institute for Empowerment of Persons with Visual Disabilities (NIEPVD), Dehradun; Swami Vivekanand National Institute of Rehabilitation Training and

Research (SVNIRTAR), Cuttack; Pt Deendayal Upadhyaya National Institute for People with Physical Disabilities, Delhi and National Institute for Empowerment of People with Multiple Disabilities (NIEPMD), Chennai. Some of these institutions also have regional centres around the country.

Some of the activities that these institutes carry out are conducting structured training courses; research and development in the area of disabilities; organizing conferences, seminar and workshops; consultancy; outreach programmes; community based rehabilitation etc.

National Trust

The National Trust for the Welfare of Persons with Autism, Celebral Palsy, Mental Retardation and Multiple Disabilities, a statutory body under the Ministry of Social Justice and Empowerment was created for the dissemination of the welfare schemes related to person with special needs. While being under the administrative control of the central government, it runs a number of programmes which are targeted at registered organisations (ROs) who would be the ground level implementers.

The Trust's vision statement seeks "*An inclusive society which values human diversity and enables and empowers full participation of Persons with Disability to live independently with dignity, equal rights and opportunities.*" On the other hand, its Mission Statement is to "*work towards providing opportunities for capacity development of Persons with Disability and their families, fulfilling their rights, facilitating and promoting the creation of an enabling environment and an inclusive society.*"

The Trust has a two pronged approach namely legal and welfare activities. The former is through the Local Level Committee (LLCs) at the district level which number 628. The LLCs are chaired by the District Magistrate or District Commissioners and have to meet at regular intervals. Their main role is in the appointment or removal of guardians for people with disabilities.

The welfare is undertaken through specific schemes that are operated by registered organisations (RO) which number around 550. These schemes, all of which have their unique staff requirements, funding pattern and infrastructural facility parameters have been spelt out in the subsequent paragraphs.

Disha, an early intervention and school readiness scheme of the Trust targets children under the age group of 10. This seeks to catch those children who show symptoms and need special attention. They are then put through an intervention programme which enables them to make the necessary tweaks to adjust to the environment of able bodied children.

The Vikaas day care scheme on the other hand is targeted at those above the age of 10 with the conditions of autism, celebral palsy, mental retardation and multiple disabilities. It seeks to enhance the interpersonal and vocational skills of those afflicted with these conditions. The scheme has an implicit understanding that it may be difficult for such children and adults to be integrated directly into the mainstream schools and workplaces. Therefore, it is tailored to look at how such children and adults can be provided some inputs on both strengthening their interpersonal skills and vocational training to undertake some jobs. There are numerical limits for enrolment in a Vikaas Centre with a minimum attendance requirement for being funded by the Trust. For ROs who want to implement both the Disha and Vikaas schemes, an option has been given to merge these into the Disha-cum-Vikaas Scheme (Day Care) with effect from 1 April, 2018.

Samarth is a respite care scheme that provides a respite care home to orphans, families in crisis, persons with atleast one of the four disabilities from lower income categories (below poverty line and lower income group). There are numerical limits for persons with disabilities enrolled in these centres and a fifty fifty ratio between those in the lower income group (LIG) and those above LIG with the latter paying the service charges of the centre.

Gharaunda, while being an adult care scheme provides housing and care services throughout the life of a person with the disabilities of autism, celebral palsy, mental retardation and multiple disabilities. A group facility also enhances the social interaction of these adults thereby alleviating their stress levels. The scheme also has a numerical limit of 26 persons with disabilities and has to maintain the 1:1 ratio of those in LIG and those above it. In line with the earlier schemes, the ROs were given an option to merge both these schemes into the Samarth-cum-Gharounda scheme on 1 April, 2018.

The Niramaya Health Insurance Scheme is designed to provide an affordable health insurance to the persons with autism, celebral palsy, mental retardation and multiple disabilities. The cover is upto Rs 1 lakhs and covers hospitalization, both corrective surgeries and non-surgical, OPD treatment including for dental, ongoing therapies, alternative medicine and transportation costs. The scheme requires a person to approach one of the registered organisations for enrollment. Even for parents who are guardians, they need to get a guardian certificate.

Sahyogi scheme has the objective of providing training for the caregivers of persons afflicted with disabilities. There are two levels, primary and advanced which cater to both parents of such children or even for NGOs and other organisations who work in this field. This is undertaken through Care Associate Cells (CACs) which are to be set up by the registered organisations (ROs) with adequate infrastructure and human resources. The primary course is a 3 month module prepared by the Rehabilitation Council of India (RCI) which caters to areas such as family needs, health, nutrition, basic management in activities of daily living, assistive devices and barrier free environment, orientation, mobility sensory motor stimulation and administering first aid care. On the other hand, the advanced course is of 6 months duration covering areas like language and communication (including sign language), social interactions, socio-emotional management, learning and understanding, behaviour management, managing sexuality, working with adults and administering advanced medical care including regular theoretical inputs. The trainees are to be in the age group of 18-45 years and are entitled to a stipend. The funding to the RO takes places under three heads, namely the set up cost, cost for training and reimbursement of stipend paid to trainees.

Gyan Prabha is a scheme that provides educational support for the person with disabilities to pursue both graduation and professional education courses as well as vocational training for being employed. The Trust provides direct funding which would normally cover fees, transportation, books and out of pocket expenses. However, the Scheme was discontinued from January, 2018.

Prerna is a marketing assistance initiative targeted at marketing and distribution of products made by people with disabilities. The registered organization, with predominant employees being those with disabilities, are also provided funds for participation in exhibitions and fairs at the national, regional, state and district levels. The funding pattern is in three components namely participation fee in the event, 10% in incentive on sales turnover and reimbursement of design, printing and distribution of brochures.

Sambhav, a programme of aids and assisted devices for people with disabilities, works through the concept of centres established in large cities. These Sambhav centres aim to provide information and easy access to devices, appliances, aids, software etc that facilitate working of people with disabilities. Some of these include aids for daily living, mobility aids, home and workplace modifications, devices for seating and positioning, alternative and augmentative communication device, prosthetic and orthotic devices, vehicle modifications, sensory aids for vision and hearing impaired, computer access aids, recreational aids for social and cultural events and sports, and environmental controls. The funding would be in the form of a set up cost, monthly recurring costs and reimbursement for new devices added to the Sambhav centre every year.

Badhte Kadam is a social awareness campaign with an aim of creating community awareness, sensitization, social integration and mainstreaming of people with disabilities. Funds are provided to registered organizations to create awareness and conduct events under various categories like distribution of promotional material to educational, financial and medical institutes, conduct special sessions for people with disabilities, organise roadshows, conduct workshops for targeted audience, organise socially inclusive events and conduct sessions in schools to create awareness among students.

The plethora of schemes of the National Trust must be complemented. However, the crux is about the implementation and the effective monitoring of the registered organization (ROs) is a sine quo non for the success of the schemes. Secondly, with the developments in medical science, the schemes must keep pace. As people interpret the language of the regulatory framework, even common syndromes like the Down's took some time to be made part of the scheme. There must be a system of automatic addition of syndromes diagnosed around the world into the purview of the scheme. Finally, the Trust must co-ordinate with State Governments who are an important stakeholder in the implementation of the schemes.

CHAPTER FIVE

Rehabilitation Council of India

The Rehabilitation Council of India (RCI), a statutory body under Divyangjan was established in 1992 under the RCI Act, 1992. The Act spells out the objective of regulating the training policies and programmes for rehabilitation of people with disabilities and maintaining a Central Rehabilitation Register. It also includes the standardization of these programmes, prescribing minimum standards for those administering it, recognition of educational institutes running these programmes, promoting research, recognition of vocational rehabilitation centres, registration of personnel working in these institutes and all activities related to the field of rehabilitation of persons with disabilities.

The scope of the RCI Act cover four types of disabilities namely visually handicapped, hearing handicapped, locomotor disability and mental retardation. Visually handicapped have been demarcated into three sub categories namely total loss of sight or visual sight < 6/60 or 20/200 in the better eye or limitation of field of vision subtending and angle of degree or worse. For the hearing handicapped the deafness has been defined as 70 decibels or more in the better ear or total loss in both ears. The locomotor disability pertains to the inability to move of both person or any objects on account of affliction of bones, joint, muscles or nerves. Mental retardation has been defined as arrested or incomplete development of mind of a person, specially characterized by sub-normality of intelligence.

The institutions that impart course in rehabilitation have to be registered with RCI. The process is based on inspection including evaluation of infrastructural facilities carried out by experts from RCI. As of 19 May, 2022, there were 771 institutions across the country. RCI has also standardized some 56 training programmes in which certificates, diplomas, degrees, PG diploma, masters, M.Phil or Psy.D can be given.

The rehabilitation professionals need to be registered with RCI for practicing in India. There are 16 categories of professionals defined by RCI namely speech therapists, clinical psychologists, hearing aid technicians, rehabilitation engineers and technicians, special teachers, vocational counselors, multipurpose rehabilitation therapists, speech technicians, rehabilitation psychologists, rehabilitation social workers, rehabilitation practitioners in mental retardation, orientation and mobility specialists, community based rehabilitation professionals, rehabilitation counselors, prosthetics and orthotics and rehabilitation workshop managers. RCI is empowered under the Act to add any other category of professionals to this list. As of 2022, nearly 1.7 lakh professionals have been registered by RCI.

The RCI (Standards of Professional Conduct, Etiquette and Code of Ethics of Rehabilitation Professionals) Regulations 1998 govern the standards to be maintained by the rehabilitation professionals. Some of the activities proscribed or liable for being declared as infamous conduct for such professionals are exaggeration of the forecasting of the course of disease, maintaining indecent or illicit relationship with the subject, using harsh or rough language with subject, charging exorbitant fee or taking undue advantage of the person with disabilities, not undertaking or neglecting rehabilitation.

Under the Continuing Rehabilitation Education (CRE) programme, the RCI through training institutes conducts workshops, seminars and conferences including in virtual mode in the field of disability rehabilitation and special education. The primary purpose is to update the skills and knowledge of professionals, personnel and master trainers. These training programmes are monitored by fourteen Zonal Coordination Committees (ZCC), spread throughout the country.

While the norms and guidelines for CRE were published in August, 2018, the revised guidelines for CRE Webinar was published on September, 2020. There are eligibility conditions for institutions conducting such programmes such as 5 years experience in conducting RCI programmes or 10 years experience on working with people with disabilities. The general guidelines prescribe the numerical limit of trainees, topics on which the programme can be conducted and the funding available under various Heads. The funding limits are Rs 90,000 for a 5 day programme and Rs 54,000 for a 3 day programme with individual component breakdowns too given.

The Webinar Guidelines of 2020 prescribe a criteria for the platform chosen, presence of a dedicated technical team, duration of the webinar, evaluation criteria for the webinar, topics selected and resource persons for the same, weightage points to be granted to participants, fee to be taken, guidelines for submission of report, compilation of the proceedings, accrual of CRE points for renewal etc. In the light of the pandemic lockdowns the electronic medium of such webinars has been given priority by RCI to disseminate relevant information.

The National Board of Examination in Rehabilitation (NBER) conducts examinations in this field. This is an adjunct body of RCI and is based out of Chennai.

The RCI is thus a crucial cog in the wheel of the entire policy on people with disabilities. Its programmes and recognition of agencies and professionals is crucial to ensure that the government policies can be implemented at the ground level. The maintenance of appropriate level of standards is also an critical aspect to ensure that the delivery of services to people with disabilities is efficacious and lead to perceptible change in their lives.

National Handicapped Finance and Development Corporation (NHFDC)

NHFDC was set up in January, 1997 by the Central Government with the aim of channelizing funds to persons with disabilities through the State Channelising Agencies (SCA). It is a non-profit company wholly owned by the Government of India.

One of the schemes run by NHFDC is the Divyangjan Swavalamban Yojana (DSY) which provides concessional credit to people with disabilities. It covers activities related to income generation, pursuing higher education, pursuing vocational or skill development or purchase of assistive device. The interest rate is concessional with a further discount of 1% for women with disabilities. While there is flexibility on the type of loan, it is to be repaid in ten years and there is a stipulation of any security by

NHFDC.

NHFDC also provides credit based funding based on the broad parameters of its DSY scheme. Some of the areas of this funding are self-employment ventures, higher education, vocational training, upgradation of skills, setting of up training or facilitation centres, refinancing of state level organisations and assistance in marketing of products made by persons with disabilities. The implementing agencies are the state channelizing agencies, nominated banks and NBFCs/MFIs with whom MOUs exist. The contribution from States and implementing agencies is also required for thresholds beyond Rs 50,000/-.

The Vishesh Microfinance Yojana (VMY) is another scheme where the NHFDC has a tie up with the last level microfinancers to reach the targeted population. The micro-finance institutions (MFI) are the last connectivity for funding people with disabilities and NHFDC funds 90% of the costs. The interest spread for the implementing agencies cannot exceed 8% and hence this works out to be more expensive than the other schemes of NHFDC. The repayment is stringent with a 3 year period and full security such as bank guarantee or post dated cheques or exclusive first use hypothecation are also required. Moreover, there is a threshold limit of Rs. 60.000/- for lending.

A unique scheme of NHFDC is to provide a commercial vehicle loan for the specially abled people. This vehicle is then leased to fleet operators through the NHFDC Foundation who take on the responsibility for maintenance, upkeep, yearly insurance payments, recovering monthly lease rentals, repayment of the original loan, other administrative costs and transfer of the amount to the beneficiary bank. This provides a regular source of income for the specially abled. The residual value of the vehicle at the end of the loan is another source of income in this business model. However, in a variant, this residual value can be loaded in the monthly income, but then at the end of the loan tenure, the vehicle is transferred to the fleet owner.

NHFDC also has a scheme of having portable micro skilling training centres which provides skill training facilities for various trades specific to a geographical location. They are to be uniformly designed, accessible, have quality support facilities and be equipped with the requisite machinery for undertaking training. These are known as Swavalamban Kendras and have a standard design, area and specifications. A 30x10 feet Kendra can provide skill training to around 100 specially abled people every year. Concessional credits and training grants are provided by NHFDC to specially abled people who want to run them. They also provide grant in aid for running the centre for 4 years. The NHFDC Foundation provides the guidance, support and handholding to the specially abled persons to run the Kendras.

The NHFDC is another key aspect to ensure the availability of finance at competitive rates to the people with disabilities. This facilitates the operation of enterprises by them so as to earn a livelihood and be financially independent. Moreover, there is a distinct possibility that the growth of such enterprises would lead to greater employment of PwDs as well as activities concerning the inclusion of them into mainstream.

Global Celebrities with Disabilities

Many of the talented persons in our history who went onto establish repute in their fields had some form of disabilities. They somehow overcame societal prejudices and other obstacles in their way to carve a niche in the areas of their specialization. In the less severe cases, it has been one of dyslexia which had led to learning disabilities and blurring of speech. However, serious impairments have also afflicted many such geniuses. One of the prime reasons put forth that these people overcome the adversities, was their ability to focus their energies into their abled functions which more than compensated the disabilities they had. Let us dwell into the history of some of them starting off with scientists and physicists, many of whom were also inventors.

Ironically, the man who many argue was probably the most intelligent human being ever to walk on this planet had disabilities. Albert Einstein, the scientist who is credited with the General Theory of Relativity and the law of photo-electric effect had a learning disability ostensibly referred to as dyslexia on account of which he could not speak till the age of three. In his letters, he has mentioned that *"Words or language, as they are written or spoken, do not seem to play any role in my mechanism of thought"*. He faced hurdles in arithmetic, though he was strong in geometry, probably one of his fortes of his area of research. Moreover, his writing skills were also suspect. Once he mentioned to Robert Shankland, a fellow physicist that *"Writing is difficult, and I communicate this way very badly"*. While talking about his thought process, he mentioned that *"Thoughts did not come in any verbal formulation. I very rarely think in words at all. A thought comes, and I may try to express it in words afterwards"*. There were some doubts also of the Asperger Syndrome which possible justifies some of his traits of being socially aloof but these were never proven beyond doubt.

Thomas Alva Edison, the man who invented the electric bulb was born with learning disabilities and could not read until the age of twelve. His reading skills were also very mediocre due to his condition of what some say was dyslexia. He lost his hearing too possibly on account of an incident where his ears were pulled while being lifted onto a train carriage. Many experts have speculated that he also had the attention deficit hyperactivity disorder (ADHD) which primarily led to his learning abilities being curtailed. He is attributed to the saying that genius is 1%

inspiration and 99% perspiration.

A similar learning disability also afflicted the inventor of the telephone, Alexander Graham Bell. His mother and wife were both deaf and this made him work on alternate means of communication. His condition is also considered by many to be dyslexia.

The famous physicist Stephen Hawkings had the Amyotrophic Lateral Sclerosis (ALS) or the Lou Gehrigs Syndrome that confined him to a wheelchair, especially towards the end of his life. It is the progressive degeneration of motor neurons in the brain that leads to muscle atrophy. Born an able bodied person, he was diagnosed with the motor neuron disease at the age of twenty one when his speech blurred and he had difficulty walking. He completely lost his speech in a life-saving operation and had to depend on a device called the equalizer to communicate. He is credited with pathbreaking discoveries on the big bang theory, black holes, quantum theory etc. He lived till the age of 76, a rare occurrence for someone with ALS and who was given just two more years to live by doctors when diagnosed at the age of 21. His famous quote on disability was *"Concentrate on things your disability does not prevent you doing well and don't regret the things it interferes with. Don't be disabled in spirit, as well as physically."*

There were a number of famous artistes who had some disability. We start off with John Milton, the English poet who went blind at the age of fourty three. Many suspect that this was due to bilateral retinal detachment or glaucoma. He had a chequered family, friend and political life with one challenge after the other. However, it was after he lost sight that he managed to pen his magnus opus *"Paradise Lost"* following it up with a sequel *"Paradise Regained"*. These are considered as masterpieces of English poetry.

Ludwig Van Beethoven, arguably the greatest music composer of all time became deaf. Interestingly, he was dyslexic and had poor learning and mathematical skills. He began getting deaf at the age of thirty which further exacerbated his social aloofness. He is said to have written that *"I must confess that I lead a miserable life. For almost two years I have ceased to attend any social functions, just because I find it impossible to say to people: I am deaf. If I had any other profession, I might be able to cope with my infirmity; but in my profession it is a terrible handicap"*. Nevertheless, it was in this period that despite his behavioural quirks, he composed some of his greatest works. Some of his aides had said that he actually used a pencil to feel the vibrations of the piano and hence get a feel of the notes of his compositions. Not surprisingly, most of his later compositions after he became deaf were of low notes.

One of the greatest painters and sculptors, Michelangelo is suspected to have both gout and osteo-arthritis. It severely affected his profession in use of the hands for painting, chiselling and hammering. Some say that he was overworked and this lead to his condition.

The Spanish portrait painter Francisco Goya is believed to have suffered neurological problems that manifested in headaches, dizziness, hearing loss, sight loss and mobility. The treatment of syphilis through mercury and exposure to lead from the paints he used are suspected to have aggravated the situation. He suffered from depression and weight loss and eventually became deaf.

The impressionist painter Vincent Van Gogh had temporal lobe epilepsy and a bipolar disorder. Many believed it was on account of a brain lesion. He was being treated for seizures and many believed that the medication led to the yellow spots which manifested in most of his painting depicting yellow hues of nature. His bipolar disorder got manifested in the intermittent phases where he would churn out a number of works followed by a phase of depression.

Another British poet, Lord Byron had a club foot which was a congenital disability. He went to establish himself as one of the great poets of his era.

We now look at political leaders and thinkers who were afflicted with some disability or the other. Beginning with the United States, the first president George Washington had a learning disability with poor grammatical skills on account of which he could barely write. The other Presidents who had learning disabilities, including dyslexia were Thomas Jefferson, Dwight Eisenhower, Woodrow Wilson and John Kennedy. Abraham Lincoln, the 16th President was suspected to have had the Marfan Syndrome which led to him having phases of depression including suicidal tendencies. President Franklin Roosevelt contracted polio at the age of 39 but he tried to hide this from public view. Both President Clinton and Reagan had hearing impediments. The current incumbent Joe Biden has a speech disorder which has led to his stuttering.

Christopher Reeve, the Hollywood actor who became famous for his portrayal of Superman had a horse riding accident which paralysed him from neck downwards. He spent a lot of time on generating awareness of spinal cord injuries and funding research. He had famously said *"Once you choose hope, anything's possible"*.

Helen Keller was a blind and deaf author and activist who had published twelve books. She had once said *"A bend in the road is not the end of the road. Unless you fail to make the turn."*

There have been a number of specially abled motivational speakers who have changed our very perception of disability. Nick Vujicic who was afflicted with the tetra-amelia syndrome and had no limbs has been one of the most famous of such speakers. He is quoted as saying that *"I honestly didn't think miracles could ever come from my broken pieces, and I was disabled in fear that my dreams would always remain as dreams. Don't give up on you, don't give up on God, don't give up on love."*

All these celebrities highlight one important aspect. They never allowed their disability to hinder their work and focused on their abled physiological and mental faculties. As Stephen Hawking famously said

"Disability need not be an obstacle to success".

CHAPTER EIGHT

Indian Celebrities with Disabilities

Even in the case of India, there are a number of inspirational stories of people with special abilities having carved a niche in their respective fields. US President Theodore Roosevelt's quote, *"Believe you can and you are halfway there"*, aptly sums up the incredible achievements of these people in the face of adversities.

we have the danseuse and actress Sudha Chandran who is an exponent of the classical Bharatnatyam dance. At the young age of 17, she had a car accident and on account of gangrene build up, had to get a leg amputated. She showed a firm resolve and through the prosthetic Jaipur foot managed to restart her professional career in dance within 3 years of that accident in 1984. It catapulted her to being one of the most famous Bharatnatyam dancers of the country. She also acted in films and TV shows carving a niche in these fields. She even won a National Film Award for her role in the movie Mayuri. Her story is one of grit and determination. However, unfortunately, she was at the receiving end of an incident in October, 2021 when she was asked by the security personnel at an airport frisking to remove her prosthetic limb. This was indeed unnerving and humiliating for her due to which she made an appeal to the authorities for allowing people with disabilities to have easier security checks based on some identification like I cards.

Some others in the entertainment industry who had disabilities were the actress Jyoti Amge who had a genetic disorder called achondroplasia. She never grew and was thus only 62.8 centimetres in height. Abhishek Bachchan, the actor had dyslexia at the age of nine but managed to overcome this as his career in the entertainment industry progressed. Hrithik Roshan, another famous actor had to overcome stammering issues with speech therapy sessions at a young age. He however, overcame these and carved a niche in the entertainment industry. Rana Daggubati, a famous actor who starred in the superhit Bahubali series is blind in one eye. However, this has not stopped him for being one of the top performers in the industry.

Dr Suresh Advani, one of India's top oncologists was afflicted with polio at the age of eight. He pioneered the hematopoietic stem cell transplantation in the country. Another famous doctor who contracted polio was Dr Satendra Singh who then went onto become an activist with his group *"Infinite Ability"* going on to make public places disabled friendly.

Ravindra Jain was a visually impaired music director and singer. He rendered compositions for many Hindi films that went onto become gross earners.

Dr Jaipal Reddy, a politician was afflicted with polio and confined to a wheelchair. He was a cabinet minister who handled a variety of portfolios. His constituency was in the state of Telangana.

Lal Advani was a visually challenged bureaucrat and social worker. He specialized as a music teacher, medical assistant and braille tutor. He was at the helm in the National Institute of Visually Handicapped and undertook a lot of pioneering work including running a school for the blind. He was involved in the framing of the PwD Act, 1995 and the RCI Act 1999. He was an advisor in the Rehabilitation Council of India.

Rambhai Patel was a visually challenged cooperative banker who later became an independent candidate from Valsad. He had worked on rehabilitation of blind students and upliftment of tribals in Valsad.

The work of these Indian personalities in their respective fields has been creditable. They have not only created awareness about the abilities of PwD but also done a lot of welfare activities targeted at them. They have definitely created an attitudinal change in the abled bodied persons.

CHAPTER NINE

Transport accessibility – Reality in India

The reality of PwD in India has been much talked about. Despite the overall legal framework and efforts of the government to create a palpable change in the administration of schemes and attitudinal change, there is a still a lot of work remaining.

We start with the Indian Railways. There is no doubt that the institution has come a long way in addressing the needs of the specially abled. This has also been spurred by the public pressure manifested in the form of press reporting and complaints filed. Some of these are the facilities in railway stations for physically and visually impaired as well as concession in fares for those holding requisite certificates.

While all this is laudable, there is still some way to go on this front. Firstly, the very overcrowded and chaotic atmosphere in a station can be scary for an abled bodied person. While disabled friendly structures exist, only the end platforms have ramps where wheel chairs can be directly sent to platforms. If one has to go to the mid platforms, the stairs are the only means wherein the person and the wheelchairs have to be lifted up and down. While markings for the visually challenged exist in many stations, their usability with the all the encroachments on the platforms remains suspect. The doors of trains remain narrow and the climb from the platform to the train is not easy for a physical disability. The state of the bathrooms is another area that needs to be addressed. Even for a normal abled person, the use is a challenge. The seats are also not disabled friendly, being too narrow and there is no space to park a wheelchair.

However, one must give credit to the metros in the major cities of India. They have provided infrastructure which is fairly disabled friendly such as lifts, escalators, ramps, markings for visually impaired, special seats inside the coaches, verbal announcements etc. This is also on account of the newly created infrastructure wherein it was possible to build in all these features.

Air travel is definitely more friendly for the disabled than the other modes of transport in the country. However, there have been cases of harassment of specially abled even involving famous people. We have already dwelt on the security check of the famous actress and danseuse Sudha Chandran who was asked to take out her prosthetic foot.

Another incident that comes to light is one of 7 May, 2022 when Indigo airlines denied boarding to a differently abled child who was travelling on its route from Ranchi to Hyderabad. The passengers narrated that there was an altercation between the family of the child and the ground staff after which the special child was not allowed to board. Indigo's claim was that it was the best possible decision under the circumstances as the boy was in a state of panic. The DGCA in its internal fact finding mission had hauled up the airline stating that the handling of a special needs child was inappropriate. A notice was also submitted to the airline indicating non-conformance to its regulations. Even the Civil Aviation Minister had stated that there is zero-tolerance policy for such behavior and appropriate action would be taken.

The Civil Aviation Requirements (CAR) Section 3, Series M Part 1 regulations of February, 2014 pertain to the *"Carriage by Air - Persons with Disability and/ or Persons with ReducedMobility"*. Para 4.1.35 of these regulations states that *"Before refusing carriage to any person on the basis of disability, the airline shall specify in writing the basis of such refusal indicating its opinion that transportation of such persons would or might be inimical to the safety of flight"*. This would have been the basis for refusing the passenger with special needs. However, based on this incident, subsequently, the DGCA issued guidelines on 3rd June, 2000 adding a new para 4.1.35 stating that *"Airlines shall not refuse carriage of any person on the basis of any disability. However, in case, an airline perceives that the health of such a passenger may deteriorate in-flight, the said passenger will have to be examined by a Doctor- who shall categorically state the medical condition and whether the passenger is fit to fly or not. After obtaining the medical opinion, the Airline shall take the appropriate call"*.

Basically, this still provides a window to the airline to deny access based on the medical opinion. While one could look at arguments at both sides of the fence on whether the airline acted in the right way or not, it is important to understand that the entire issue is larger than that and is of access being provided to disabled persons to lead a life of dignity. In a country like India where there is significant apathy to a special needs person, we need to send the right message to the service providers on how to implement the policies related to people with disabilities. It was also heartening to note that many passengers supported the right of the child to travel. Indigo's arguments of the child being in a state of panic does not cut much ice since in such verbal duels, any normal person could get into a state of agitation and lose his cool. Moreover, such children need a kid glove approach and unless they are given the space and kept in a tranquil environment, a panic is likely to set in. Moreover, it is important that the boarding of such special needs passengers is undertaken first in a calmer environment before letting in the hordes of other passengers. All this is part of the protocol for handling such passengers. As for the importance of the airline to stick to time schedules, one must adopt a more pragmatic approach in such cases. The top management of Indigo which is probably monitoring such delays and gauging the performance of its employees on that must also be ready to tolerate delays in such special cases. After all if every service provider denies boarding on this excuse, how will the special needs person ever travel, whether for treatment or any other purpose. Finally a fine of Rs 5 lakhs was levied on the airline for this behavior with the hope that this deters them and other airlines from a repeat. On the issue of the amended DGCA provision for seeking a medical opinion, one can only hope that this provision is not misused for denying access to the specially- abled.

When one looks at road transport, the situation is not too rosy. While some of the buses have open spaces for parking wheelchairs, only a few low floor buses have been introduced in some cities like Delhi. Hence, access for wheelchairs is still an issue in most buses around the country. Moreover, the bus stands are not accessible in many cases and the overall experience is not disabled friendly.

In the case of other public transport such as cabs and autos, there is literally no disabled friendly feature, worth the name. There is ample scope to look at some features like inbuilt ramps, space for foldable wheelchairs, verbal communication devices etc.

While India has made some progress, the accessibility in transport is still one of the key impediments that hamper the free movement of PwD's. This is important if one needs to ensure their employment and financial independence. The enforcement mechanism would need to be strengthened too especially where the created infrastructure has been rendered ineffective due to misuse and encroachment.

CHAPTER TEN

Personal Experience

There is none who can appreciate this subject better than the parents of a special child. The spectrum of emotion range from euphoria in observing the child do or say something that it hadn't from birth to outright exasperation when the child expresses some inner frustration that is not fathomable to an abled person.

Aptly, a saying goes *"As a special needs parents, we don't have the power to make life fair, but we do have the power to make life joyful."*

When my second daughter who had a normal birth had a floppy head at the age of around 6 months, there was a suspicion that something was amiss. However, both of us never took it too seriously, since she was an active child blabbering a lot with a good grasp, even pulling my father's hair when he held her. The floppiness was what first made us take her to a pediatrician who suspected neural issues asking us to consult some hospital. So began our sojourn with hospitals in the capital, including the most sought after government ones. However, a visit there to the pediatric genetics division was an eye opener. Not only was it like an overcrowded railway platform with mothers coming from far corners of the country holding their little ones in their laps, with the latter crying and howling. It shocked us and made my wife cringe at even going in. I wondered as to why our health system was so overburdened and centralized. Couldn't we open more such hospitals and decentralize it?

However, what was in store for us even shook us further. The poor doctors were so overburdened with the flow of patients that they could hardly give enough time to each case that had its own complexity. It was like just listening amidst the sea of distractions and noise. Even the most tranquil medical professional could get spooked and what more can one think of other than providing some advise at the spur of the moment or asking for some additional tests to be done. People say that the sheer spectrum of cases that these medical professionals see provides them with the experience of a lifetime. However, to play the devil's advocate, such a claustrophobic environment day in and day out could well work the other way round by rupturing the interest that the professional may have in the field. Nevertheless, this is not the time to get into what doctors think but more on the conditions that they have to work in.

One incident that both of us still remember is the muscle biopsy that they asked us to get done for my child. We thought it best to get it done in the hospital itself which was the country's premier institution. However, what was in store for us was a shock. My wife who was a medical professional wanted to go in the theatre, but she was denied, a move which I think was correct. However, the biopsy was done largely by some interns who to put it squarely, made a mess of it. The scars of that are still visible in my daughter nearly 16 years after that process. Nothing came out from the report though except for those forgettable memories as we sat in anguish in that temporary ward.

The suspicion pointed to what we were told was celebral palsy. We did some research and found out that this was a neurological disorder which affected both the nervous system as well as physical capability of the patient. A brain scan which revealed some white matter only heightened the suspicion. The process of the brain scan was another experience since my daughter refused to lie motionless and had to be given some sedatives. However, in the absence of any conclusive evidence, we were left in the lurch. It was taking a toll on us and we realized that not much could come out of our visits.

We then tried one of the top private hospitals in the country where all the reports were examined. Strangely, however, the doctor was in awe of the government hospital where we had shown my daughter. He literally swore by the latter's diagnosis and did not offer any additional clue on the issue. This was indeed frustrating for us and there came a point when we did curse the medical system at home. A parental outburst, out of the lack of any credible information on the child, let alone the treatment.

We did try some online opinions sending the reports but there was little progress and clue on the syndrome. Lots of advise started pouring in about taking her to this place or that place in the country. However, what kept us from doing so was the hunch that if they could not diagnose her in the premier hospitals in the capital, there was little hope elsewhere. The opinions received did not spark any optimism and some sought further tests. We didn't want to go through all the agony again.

It is important to try to understand the thought process of parents of such special children. While we wouldn't bracket ourselves into the zone of desperation, we did feel a bit despondent. The thoughts that may creep up in most parents would be what happens to the child after us. Who will take care of the child and isn't it unreasonable to put the burden on the older sibling who would have a life of her own? The craziest wish that some parents have in such situations is to wish that they outlived the special child, something that neither had any control over.

Anyhow, it is in the wave of these emotions that even the most educated of parents can enter the zone of irrationality. No shame in admitting that we were also not bereft of it. One source of us indicated that there was a person who can treat all these disorders and came to the capital irregularly from his base in the eastern part of the country. Not one of those typical religious seers who claim to have a cure for anything and everything, but a middle class man who claimed to have patented an oil which could work miracles.

I must admit that I was not impressed in our first meeting and did have suspicion on the efficacy of whatever that oil was. There were a number of old people with joint issues who were there as also one with a genetic disorder, more like Downs Sydrome. The person was supremely confident of curing the condition after examining my daughter. However, we decided to give it a try as allopathy hadn't provided us any clues. So we shelled out some moolah and started the session. It was primarily rubbing of oil on my daughter's back and the subsequent massage. It went on for some months but we did not see any result and finally gave up. However, what really upset me that despite my apprehensions, there was a feeling of having fallen victim to an act of desperation. I wondered on how an educated person could fall into such a trap without getting into the scientific rationality of it. But it is basically about the human emotion bordering on hope and willingness to experiment with whatever comes across.

What made us go there despite the suspicion? It is finally a matter of hopelessness for parents of such children and how vulnerable we become at such moments. For us being financially stable, it wasn't much of a drain but I shudder to think of those parents who may have to shell out their savings to undertake treatment for such children. It must be nightmarish for them and given their precarious financial condition, it could easily unnerve anyone. No wonder you have a plethora of quacks and miracle cure masters exploiting this situation.

We did try some other techniques such as Reiki which I had some knowledge. But this also did not work out.

Of course, this incident taught us to be more circumspect and rational when it came to the treatment of our daughter. We also realised an important trait that we should not be overwhelmed with the situation and start cursing the imponderables around us. Not sure of the other parents, but such situations also makes one more attached to the special child.

CHAPTER ELEVEN

Swiss Experience

Finally, in all this exasperation to get our daughter diagnosed, we slowly got into a shell realizing that medical science in the country had not developed to the extent in this esoteric field. It also dawned on us that even with a diagnosis; there was no certainty of a cure. Nevertheless, it would have given us some modicum of comfort of knowing what had led to the situation of my daughter.

Fortunately, an official posting to Geneva in Switzerland came my way in 2010 at the Permanent Mission of India to the WTO. We decided to take her for a relook. The journey was not easy since she was addicted to music and without the songs, she would throw a tantrum. Moreover, it was not a direct flight and the stopover was long. We had to be beside her and put an earphone on her to calm her. Must say that the experience at Frankfurt airport which was our first stopover port was vastly different than the Delhi airport. The airport security and the crew were aware of the special needs of the child and were well trained and helpful in all the steps including security clearance. At the Delhi airport, it was a bit of apathy of the ground staff but the Air India crew were definitely more sensitive. All it requires is some sensitization to people with special needs. The other passengers were curious but one could make out from the expression that it was more about treating us like normal people. The best part was that nobody was trying to intervene unless really needed.

Once in Geneva, we felt a lot more comfortable since the city was more disabled friendly. Easier to take my daughter for walks, no encroachments, walkers and runners realizing the need to keep their distance and giving us space, sensitivity of vehicle drivers when it came to pedestrian crossings etc. The buses were low floored for prams to be taken in and adequate space to place these prams. The passengers were also more caring towards such children. It was the first time we realized how life was so different for specially abled people back home. Some say it may be the population pressure but it is more about how people are trained for behaving towards them.

Another incident which I would like to relate to in the city was when I participated in the Geneva marathon in 2011. Not surprisingly since UNICEF was the chief sponsor, there were many specially abled children being wheeled by volunteers from specific points of the course. I remember one such encounter between the 25th and 30th kilometre of the race when a group of excited kids were being wheeled by some volunteer runners. There were a varied set of cases including those with Down's syndrome and some visually challenged. The others running around them were giving them a hi-fi despite almost on the verge of hitting the wall as they say in the gruelling distance. It was too emotional for many like me who had a light banter with them in broken French. It is outdoor social events like this that brings out their raw emotion after being confined to their homes for most of their lives. One can make out that a proper socially interactive environment can give them the requisite boost in morale.

It is interesting to note that in such sporting events in India too such as the Mumbai Marathon, there are some organizations which get some of the specially abled persons to join in and enjoy the atmosphere

----

Phelan Mcdermid Syndrome (PMS)

We spent quite a while in Geneva taking our daughter to some pediatricians and geneticists. One of our first encounter was that of a pediatrician whose clinic was on the outskirts of the town. It was a small clinic and we reached dot at the appointment time. There was some apprehension since we had a general impression that we might not be wiser than what the situation was on our daughter's condition.

When the doctor first saw the child, he was curious. We showed him all the reports which he went through in detail. There was a language barrier but then we had a colleague who helped us out. Once the doctor had gone through the papers in details including the negative biopsy and the inconclusive brain scan report, he started examining the child.

He was in for a shock, since on account of the absence of music my daughter began to cry and whine. He seemed a bit perplexed and did not how to handle the situation as the patient began to show reluctance to any examination. Both of us had to help in calming our daughter down. What struck me was that he may not have come across such cases and would not have prepared himself for the same. This only added to our despondency over whether we would ever get a clue on the ailment in Geneva.

However, he made us carry out some further tests for clarity. After a couple of visits, he somehow honed onto the fact that this could be a genetic disorder and asked us to consult the genetics division of a cantonal hospital. He put in a word to the doctors there and we were given a suitable appointment.

We went to this hospital and met the head of the genetics division. He seemed curious and had a couple of his interns too to examine our daughter. Moreover, he was very friendly to us and spoke in English. The entire family history was checked and like a master craftsman, he examined each of the reports and discussed extensively with his students. It was a lengthy two hour conversation and we were pleasantly surprised at his teams commitment and methodical process to get to the root of all this. Back home, even a five minute appointment is considered long given the queues of patients waiting outside to barge in. He finally took a blood sample of our daughter. He clearly articulated his line of thought stating that he suspected a genetic disorder for which he would need to take the sample and carry out permutations and combinations to find out the suspected disorder.

We waited anxiously for a week to hear from the hospital. It was then that I got a call from the doctor whose tone was like the *"eureka"* moment of a major discovery. He was so excited exclaiming that he had found the syndrome and asked us to come over on a particular date. We went in all excited ourselves and here again we had a long session with the doctor and his students.

He patiently explained to us that our daughter had what was known as the Phelan Mcdermid Syndrome or PMS wherein a particular gene called the shank gene was missing in her chromosome. The function of this gene was still not deciphered and it had led to the condition that my daughter was in. His students were also excited at the discovery since such cases would have been rare in their medical careers too. To put it bluntly, both of us were relieved that the diagnosis has been finally done after the hours of fruitless running around we had done of various hospitals and clinics in India. There was hope too that there could be a cure to this syndrome. However, alas we got to know that there is no therapy known to cure it. All what could be done was to manage it.

Nevertheless, we joined a Facebook group on PMS. It was a relief for us and some early communication on the group provided us a ray of hope that we could communicate with parents who had such special kids. The group was founded by the two geneticists who had discovered PMS.

The next question that propped up was the source of this missing gene. It had to be one of the parents and he suggested that we give our blood samples too. After we gave our samples, I had to return to India to drop my wife and daughter. After I came back to Geneva, it was nearly a month after which I got a call from the hospital to visit them. In the discussions with the Head, I was told that my daughter got the condition from me. I had the shank gene in the wrong pair of chromosome which is known by the condition of balanced translocation. This surprisingly is very common and there is a 50% probability that the offspring will not have the gene. Well, then began the query of where I had got it from. Only my mother was alive and we decided to get her tested. However, in all the bureaucratic paperwork, we couldn't get the permission to get her tested in Geneva. I didn't want to subject her to any tests in India given our experience. Nothing against our medical system which possibly has some of the best brains but just about the exasperation from our previous experience.

While we remained content that the diagnosis was done, the fact remains that there is no cure. However, for parents like us, it provided some solace that we knew what the issue was. We have now learnt to live with it. During another of our social media searching, we came across another couple in Hyderabad who also had a child with PMS. It was not surprisingly diagnosed in Australia.

We just wonder as to why our genetics research has not kept pace with our progress in other fields of medicine. This is surely something for our policy makers to ponder on. One school of thought is the sheer volume of cases and hence the priority being placed on treatment of able bodied people.

However, what we learnt from all this experience is that it is important for us to allocate adequate more funding for such new syndromes and develop the entire genetics divisions of our top hospitals. One school of thought may be the finances warranted but unless these fields are developed, one cannot make progress on the treatment of such cases. It would also open the avenue for looking at earning revenues through medical tourism in this niche field sometime in the future.

CHAPTER THIRTEEN

Paralympics

Perhaps the ability of the physically and mentally challenged persons has never been more starkly on display than in the Paralympics which is held alongside the Olympic Games. It brings to the fore the unique ability of the participants with varying degree of difficulty in their events. The Games has proven the adage *"don't judge a disability only by its visibility"*.

Oscar Pistorius, a South African athlete who ran with artificial legs had said *"You are not disabled with the disabilities you have, you are able by the abilities you have"*. Pistorius, had his feet amputated due to a congenital defect. He ran the sprint races in an artificial limb and was famously known as the blade runner. Being unable to qualify for the Summer Olympic Games of 2000, he did manage to qualify for the 2012 Games, being the first amputee runner to do so. He ran both the quarter mile and the relay heats. Despite all the controversies in his life including a convicted case of homicide, there is no doubt that his performance as a specially abled athlete would go down in history since he competed in the Summer Olympics with abled bodied athletes.

However, it is interesting to note that while the case of Pistorius received the maximum publicity, there have been instances of disabled athletes competing and actually winning gold medals at the Olympics. George Eyser from the US won an incredible three gold medals in gymnastics using wooden legs in the 1904 Games. Carlo Orlandi, the deaf and mute boxer from Italy won the gold in the 1928 Games while Oliver Hallasy from Hungary who had an amputation below the knee was part of the gold medal water polo team in 1932 and 1936 Olympics. Karoly Takacs from Hungary with an injured hand won the shooting gold's in the 1948 and 1952 Games. Harold Connoly of the US had *"Erbs Palsy"* which is characterized by weakness of the arms and yet he won the gold in the demanding discipline of the hammer throw in 1956. Two deaf athletes, Illdijo Uljaty Rejko from Hungary in fencing and Jeffrey Float from US in swimming won golds during the Olympics of 1964 and 1984 respectively. However, one of the most amazing feats of the modern games has to be of the visually impaired Korean archer Dong-Hyun who won gold in both the 2004 and 2008 Games. In fact as stated earlier, he refused to undergo laser surgery for sight improvement since his theory was that it would affect his performance.

While the first Paralympic games were held in 1960 at Rome, the build up to this was a wheelchair archery competition for injured servicemen known as the Stoke Mandeville Games which was held in 1948 alongside the London Olympic Games. It was conceived by Dr Ludwig Guttman who ran the Stoke Mandeville spinal injuries centre and had an aim of using sports as a means for recovery from spinal injuries and rehabilitation into mainstream society. While the Rome Games started with 400 athletes from 23 countries, the first Winter Paralympics were held in 1976.

The International Sports Organisation for the Disabled (ISOD) which was formed in 1964 provided an opportunity for para-athletes to compete. It also pushed for getting in blind and amputee athletes in the 1976 Toronto Paralympics and those with celebral palsy in the 1980 Arnhem Games. The International Paralympic Committee (IPC) which organizes these Games came into existence in September, 1989. The IPC had an agreement with the International Olympic Committee (IOC) on account of which the Games have been held in the same city as the Olympic Games from the 1988 Summer Games in Seoul in the 1992 Winter Games in Albertville.

There are 23 disciplines cutting in the Summer Games with some of these based on the level of disability of the athletes. On the Winter Games sides, there are four disciplines namely para Alping skiing, para Nordic skiing, para snowboard and para ice hockey.

The classification is carried out for different disciplines depending on the type and nature of impairment. For example in the case of athletics track and jumps, there are 29 impairment types, 7 classes for wheelchair racing and 3 classes for race running. In the case of throws, there are 19 classes of standing throws, 31 impairment types and 11 classes of seated throws. All of this checking is carried out through medical documentation.

Apart from Pistorius's incredible feat, there have been some exceptional para athletes who have shone in their disciplines despite their physical and mental challenges. The most accomplished Paralympian ever is Trischa Zorn who has won an incredible 41 golds and a total of 55 medals. A swimmer, she was blind from birth and competed in 3 categories over a wide span of the Games from 1980 to 2004. Her array of events which included the relays ranged from 50 meters to 400 meters. With such a rich haul, she has been the most dominant athlete of these Games.

Another notable achievement has been of Bebe Vio, the only fencer on a wheelchair without arms and legs. She won the gold in her category in the 2016 Rio Games which is stated to be one of the greatest achievements of the Games when one puts in perspective her level of disability.

Zheng Tao from China, known as the *"armless wonder"* smashed the world record in the 100 metres backstroke in the 2012 London Paralympic Games. He also won in the 2016 Games in Rio.

Shingo Kuneida, the Japanese paralympian has been a star in the wheelchair tennis discipline. He won the gold in the 2008 Beijing Games.

India's performance at the Paralympics was nothing much to write home about until the 2021 edition held in Tokyo. It was a rich haul of 5 golds, 8 silvers and 6 bronze medals across various disciplines in these Games. The gold medals were won by Avani Lekhra and Manish Narwal in shooting, Krishna Nagar and Pramod Bhagat in badminton and Sumit Antil in javelin throw. The latter's performance was surely the standout since he sunk his own world record five times in the competition. A lot of credit should also be given to the Suhas Yathiraj who is the District Magistrate of Gautam Buddha Nagar, Uttar Pradesh for the silver in badminton. It was a stupendous effort amidst a hectic work schedule in a sensitive and important posting.

The 17th Summer Paralympic Games in Paris would be held from 28 August to 8 September, 2024. There would be 4400 athletes who would compete in 549 events across 22 disciplines. It is interesting to note that the out of 4400 athletes, 339 would be of other gender. This is a reflection of the sensitivity to the rights of the LGBT and the inclusivity of the Games.

The 14th Winter Paralympics would be held in Milan and Cortino D'Ampezzo in Italy from 6-15 March, 2026. The six disciplines expected in these Games are alpine skiing, biathlon, cross-country skiing, ice sledge hockey, snowboarding and wheelchair curling.

The Paralympics while increasing in popularity Games after Games has put at the forefront the ability of people with disabilities. It has also made yeoman contribution to ensuring greater acceptance and inclusivity of those with these challenges. Dr Guttman would never have imagined the scale of these Games but we all owe a gratitude to him for having laid the foundation stone.

CHAPTER FOURTEEN

Ergonomics for Specially Abled Working Space

One of the key hindrances in the assimilation of the disabled into mainstream society is the absence of basic features in office working spaces and accessibility. The ergonomics of an office could be a harbinger of ensuring that we can have the specially abled persons contributing in good measure to our economic growth story. While there have been earnest efforts both in the public and private sector to create the requisite office space, there is still a lot of room for improvement.

These key features begin with exclusive parking space that provides closer access to the office; ramps for wheeling in the disabled both at the entry and exit; wide doorways which allow wheelchairs to come in; large washrooms with adequate support bars, tactile paving etc.

Picking up on these elements individually, parking space, preferably at the front of the office is a sine quo non for ensuring easy access for the specially abled into the office premises. It should preferably be near the entry ramp for disabled persons to minimize the commute. Moreover, it must be strictly enforced to be used only for those with disabilities.

The ramps at the entrance and exits would then enable access for such persons without having the need to climb stairs. There is the possibility of having separate entrances in case of abled bodied and specially abled persons. Many corporates and government offices in India do have these designated parking spaces and the requisite ramps.

The commute to the nearest lift or escalator should be hindrance free. Moreover, for the visually impaired, it is important to have tactile paving, those that have a distinctive raised surface profile. This facilitates movement of both visually impaired and sighted persons.

The escalators and lifts must be user friendly. The doors of the lift and the width of the escalators must be wide enough for access to wheelchairs. The buttons including the emergency one for the lift should be at a low height and accessible to those sitting in wheelchairs. There must be speakers as well as visual signaling for clear instructions. If there are adequate number of lifts, the one designated for specially abled should ideally be the slow moving one typically used in hospitals or for moving goods. Depending on the building structure and the number of floors, one should also explore those transparency lifts with a glass wall for clear outside view.

After one enters the specific floor, it is important to have tactile flooring there too. The floor tiles should have a firm grip and should not be slippery. The corridors must be wide enough for access for wheelchairs. Adequate hygiene and sanitation must be maintained.

If the specially abled person would be occupying cubicles, these should be big enough for a wheelchair and have adequate space for keeping office equipment and other stationery. It would be preferable that laptops are provided to specially abled persons along with other assistive devices. Even the laptops/ desktops should be suitably modified with features and requisite apps such as speaker assistance, braille keyboards etc.

In case of factory floors, the tactile flooring along with adequate sitting space are important. There must be suitable emergency switches, CCTV monitoring and backup medical team on standby.

For the services providers like the hospitality sector, there is need for safety devices in terms of the working places like kitchens. Personal safety equipment may also be needed for specially abled when working in an environment which entails customer interface.

Some of the other aspects that needs to be looked at are canteen/ cafeteria with suitable seating for the specially abled, open spaces and people for assistance. One of the crucial aspects in any working environment is of course that able bodied people must be well trained for interaction. There must be provision for wheelchairs at appropriate places. Moreover, there is a need for separate washrooms for the specially abled. In the absence of the same, specially abled specific WCs must be installed in the existing washrooms. Moreover, one would need to have washbasins low enough for people in wheelchairs to use them.

Technology has been one of the greatest boons even in this space. The use of technology based assistive devices have mushroomed and proven their usefulness. Voice based interactive office devices can be an effective tool for the specially abled. For the visually impaired, some of the devices include phones with tactile buttons, screen reading software, text to speech software with optical character recognition (OCR), large print materials, talking devices braille displays etc.

For those with autism or other related disabilities, some of the devices could be visual timers, sensor toys and social skills videos.

Therefore, it is important to give emphasis on how to make the modern office spaces ergonomically designed for those with disabilities. While it is undoubtedly the attitude of the abled people which is at the topmost of the pecking order, the use of assistive devices could significantly ameliorate the disadvantage that the specially abled people may have. We must all work towards this goal at a steady pace.

CHAPTER FIFTEEN

Skilling of People with Disabilities

Skilling is possibly one of the most important initiatives needed for the assimilation of specially abled people into the mainstream societal milieu. Vocational training for creating the right job opportunities would ensure the effective utilization of human resources and make them financially independent. It also would also reduce the fiscal pressures created due to the dependency of these specially abled people on government schemes. There are reports such as those of the World Bank which estimate that around 5-7% of GDP is foregone on account of keeping these challenged persons out of the purview of economically beneficial vocation.

The Government of India has many schemes tailored for this. We begin with the National Skill Development Corporation (NSDC). It is a non-profit public limited company with a 49% government stake that seeks to promote skill development by catalyzing development of skill development centres. The NSDC provides funding to business enterprises, companies and organisations for providing skill training. It supports skill development initiatives in with a focus on 37 identified sectors. The three main activities carried out by NSDC are funding of schemes, enabling support services and encouraging participation of private players.

Under the NSDC, the Skill Council for People with Disabilities (SCPwD) was set up in October, 2015 to fulfil the mission of mainstreaming People with Disabilities (PwD) through skill training and thereby enable them to earn a livelihood and contribute to economic development.

The Services provided by SCPwD are affiliation, training, assessment and certification. The scope covers, trainers, assessors, assessment agency, inspection agency, training partners and industry partners.

The Schemes which are relevant in this context are the Pradhan Mantri Kaushal Vikas Yojana (PMKVY), Deen Dayal Upadhyay Grameen Kaushal Yojana (DDU GKY), MSJE-SIPDA, State Missions, National

Apprentice Promotion Scheme (NAPS) etc.

This is supplemented by vocational courses offered by the National Institutes of DEPwD and their affiliate organisations like National Trust, NHFDC etc. These have already been discussed earlier.

The Ministry of Labour and Employment has 21 (as of July, 2022) vocational rehabilitation centres for handicapped (VRCH). It all began in 1968 with two centres set up in Mumbai and Hyderabad after signing of a MOU with the US government.. The VRCH in Vadodara exclusively caters to women with disabilities. There are skill training workshops (STWs) and Rural Rehabilitation Extension Centres (RRECs) with some of centres. It seeks to assess vocational and psychological needs to handicapped persons and render rehabilitation assistance. The assessment is done through interviews and the residual capacities gauged. The medical examination and then testing on various job capabilities is undertaken on the basis of which training is imparted to ensure work environment adjustment. This is supplemented with value added services like assistance for entering job market and self-employment, information on the reservations in various government agencies, sponsoring potential candidates and recommending loans to financial institutions. In additional to these centres, the

Ministry has more than 10,000 Industrial Technical Institutes (ITI's) and 1000 employment exchanges.

There are various institutes in the country like IITs and Universities affiliated to the Ministry of Human Resources Development (MHRD) that provide training courses for the specially challenged. The NGOs and private sector organisations have also undertaken a lot of training courses for the handicapped, the latter under their corporate social responsibility (CSR). The public sector undertakings (PSUs) have also done exceptional work on this front.

The Deendayal Antodaya Yojana – National Rural Livelihood Mission (DAY-NRLM), began in 2010 with a view to address rural poverty by creating sustainable livelihood opportunities. The objective is to facilitate access to credit, support for diversification and strengthening of livelihoods and access to public services. Since the target is a household, priority is given to those with a specially abled person. The Mission covers a number of aspects like training and capacity building, financial inclusion, community related activities etc. At the district level, the implementation agencies are the District Mission Management Unit (DMMU), District Rural Development Agencies (DRDA) and Panchayati Raj Institutions. At the block level, there are the Block Mission Management Unit (BMMU) while at the local level, these are the Self Help Groups (SHGs) which actually consists of around 10-20 households.

The Ministry of Urban Affairs runs the Deendayal Antodaya Yojana – National Urban Livelihood Mission (DAY-NULM). The Missions seeks to reduce poverty and vulnerability of urban households by providing gainful self-employment and skilled wage employment opportunities. The various schemes under the DAY-NULM are the Employment through Skills Training and Placement (ESTP), Self Employment Programme (SEP), Social Mobilisation and Institution Development (SMID), Support to Urban Street Vendors (SUSV), Shelter for Urban Homeless (SVH) and Capacity Building & Training (CBT). While there is no specific mention of the preferences given to people with disabilities in these schemes, the ground level operation does take into account this parameter.

The Central Government Ministries and State Governments also have their vocational training and livelihood programmes for specially abled persons.

While all these initiatives of the government are good, the challenge is to get these skilling programmes into the mainstream of our economic development. The industrial zones or parks including those that are agri based where the bulk of employment resides need to take some serious initiatives. While each unit may have its own well-oiled policy, a comprehensive skilling initiative would ensure economies of scale. It would be important for associations to take the initiative and undertake a needs assessment study. Based on this study the rough countours of demand could be predicted. It is then that one needs to dive deep into specificities with individual companies on their actual demand in terms of the nature of work. While there are general perceptions that peripheral jobs like packing could be given to specially abled persons, this is far from the truth. Case studies have proven that they can do well in a multitude of jobs given their higher levels of focus which actually overcomes the particular disability. Moreover, with increased automation, the opportunities are more given the less reliance on physical labour at the shopfloor.

Based on this demand estimation, one could then look at putting into place the specifics of the space and equipment required for this skilling. In the absence of numbers, sometimes the economies of scale may not be achieved. In such instances one could look at co-opting the other marginalized sections of society since the whole effort is about mainstreaming them. However, the success of such skilling programmes can only be measured by the linkages with the user industry and their assimilation. This final hurdle may be the most difficult one but with the right skilling, there is always the possibility of the specially abled persons turning out to be assets for the organization.

• 86 •

CHAPTER SIXTEEN

Corporate Social Responsibility

The focus of Corporate Social Responsibility (CSR) has also not been very critically focused on disability. One of the reasons for this could also be the little information available on what could be credibly done in this field. In many instances, it figures only as a footnote to the overall policy given the false perception many have.

Many companies don't have a tangible corporate policy on the subject though they do employ a number of people with some disabilities. The vast differences in the level of disability also creates a barrier for them to really chalk out a uniform strategy.

One of the possible activities could be the creation of a skill centre for disabled people. This would however have to be need specific taking into account the activities required and the availability of the manpower in the geographical vicinity. The need assessment exercise would be the first step in terms of looking at specific functions like office functions, IT systems, packaging, shop floor, monitoring and control, utilities etc. The next exercise would then be an assessment of which of these activities can be carried out by persons of specific disabilities. Subsequently, either one looks at an existing pool of people with disabilities or makes a survey of people from a specific geographic or demographic region with the assessment the number of people and their disabilities. The mapping of these activities with the persons available would then need to be carried out in a structured manner. Another exercise which may be crucial is about the need to ensure that there are adequate growth opportunities including possible transition from a blue collar to a white collar job. One must be cognizant of having a backup team of counselors to provide the requisite assistance at every stage for ensuring a smooth workplace transition. Sometimes, the most important aspect is to look at the behavioural aspects of the able bodied people who in many cases could exhibit some diffidence to the acceptability of the people with disabilities. This of course calls for sensitivity related trainings as well as refresher courses on a regular basis. In many instances, tie ups with some experts and institutions in this area would be an asset. However, these are only supplementary and there is no alternative to corporates themselves understanding their strategic needs and synchronizing their CSRs obligations effectively thereon.

We take the case of Reliance Foundation. They have a vocational training programme where they skill the differently abled persons with a view to empowering them. Employment opportunities are also provided to these persons.

The Adani Foundation houses a Adani Skill Development Center (ASDC) which in December, 2019 celebrated the skilling of 50,000 persons after nearly 3.5 years of its existence. Some of the areas where they have provided skilling are 3D printing, simulator based crane operator, welding, stitching, tailoring, handicraft, patient care. Some of the geographical areas where they work are Mundra and Bhuj in Gujarat, Godda in Jharkhand. As part of its skilling programme, ASDC also trains the specially abled and provides them employment opportunities.

Tata Trusts is the CSR wing of the Tata Group. They carry out a lot of charitable work including in the field of disability. However, it is their group companies like Titan Industries, Tanishq and Tata Motors that hire people with disabilities. Titan started hiring from 1980 onwards and can boast of 4% of their specially challenged employees.

ITC Limited, the agro processing and hospitality conglomerate has also been hiring people with disabilities. ITC-Welcomgroup has an HR policy which provides opportunities for them. However, an interesting news report of 19 July, 2022 alluded to them hiring visually impaired persons under the "Mangaldeep Sixth Sense" programme for their fragrances division. It was reported that the visually impaired had a heightened sense of smell which was an asset for the specific task at hand. Despite the large domestic demand, the essential oils market in India has limited domestic capacities and hence this is a growing sector where people with sight disability could find employment opportunities. It is believed that the company is also looking to expand this hiring to their personal care and foods divisions.

Lemon Tree hotels are a prime example of how to build in the concept of inclusivity in one's business model. Since 2007, they have been hiring people with disabilities starting with deaf employees and then expanding to those with intellectual and physical disabilities. The inclusivity also incorporates the marginalized sections of society like trans-genders, ostracized widows and acid attack victims. Nearly 20% of their workforce have some form of disability or are marginalized sections which is probably the highest ratio for any corporate. Beginning as a pilot project, they have such employees in virtually every department from front office, foods and beverages, engineering and finance departments. They have a 10 day training programme known as *"See, Smile and Greet"*. Those with Down Syndrome have a shorter 1hour per workday training to prevent being overstressed.

The model also makes business sense since they do not have to compete hard for employees in the hospitality sector unlike other chains. Moreover some of the traits on which they outscore the abled persons are being more creative, focused, solution oriented and sensitive to the needs of customers. The efficiency rate has also been markedly higher in some specific activities like room cleaning, setting of tables etc. The feedback has also been positive and the retention rate of employees is higher.

Capgemini India, which is an IT based subsidiary company of a French conglomerate is yet another example. Their disability inclusion programme is based on four principles of accessibility, career, engagement and evangelism. The last principle primarily focuses on the need to ensure the acceptability of the specially abled persons in the work environment. In terms of career, they started employing specially abled persons from 2012 onwards and has around two hundred such employees. The intake cuts across all disabilities including sight, speech, hearing, celebral palsy, epilepsy, schizophrenia etc. These persons are employed in a number of areas like accounts, technology support and software development. Capgemini also has a skilling programme known as the LEAP Inclusion Digital Academy Program for Youth with Disability in India. The ten skilling centres around the country impart training on IT skills, coding, analytics, graphic designing, programming languages etc.

Accenture, runs a programme called the *"Skills to Succeed"* initiative which provides skilling to people on business process outsourcing (BPO), hospitality, retail services and facilities management. For its specially abled employees, it runs a programme called *"PwD Champions Network"* which equips them to handle the work they carry out. There are more than 6000 people involved in this work in India. They have also loaded videos on Indian Sign Language (ISL) to equip the abled persons to interact with those who are hearing and speech challenged.

Wipro has disseminated the concept of inclusivity amongst its workforce. It undertakes merit based hiring for differently abled persons which is across all job profiles. They have formulated an internal Equal Opportunity and Reasonable Accommodation Policy. Their strategic framework CREATE (Career, Recruitment, Enablement, Accessibility, Training,

Engagement) is the principle on which the effective inclusion of employees is undertaken at WIPRO. Some of the key aspects of this policy is to ensure adequate physical infrastructure, digital infrastructure, reasonable accommodation, employee engagement and social inclusion.

IBM on the other hand has the concept of 3 A's namely Accommodation, Accessibility and Attitude. It employs specially abled people in departments such as Project Management, Consulting, Quality Assurance and Human Resources. It also carries out sensitization workshops for its employees.

While many corporates are undertaking CSR activities, the scale is still not commensurate with the number of specially abled people. The basic mindset of employing them has to change from that of being a liability to an asset due to the better development of their other faculties. One of the greatest fears that many harbor is the affect it would have on abled bodied persons. Hence, it is imperative that before embarking on such activities including skilling, it is important to school the latter into accepting the specially abled. The right approach is needed in terms of ensuring the right balance between adopting a sympathetic attitude to one where has empathy while treating them as normal persons. Without this, it would be a difficult task to create inclusivity.

CHAPTER SEVENTEEN

What India Needs?

It is clear from the previous chapters that India has a long way to go to make it a `friendly country for the specially abled. However the task is not insurmountable and needs some specific interventions at the policy level. The government has been sounding the right notes and creating the requisite infrastructure.

Robert Hansel had said *"There is no greater disability in society than the inability to see a person as more."* Hence, firstly, it is important to create an attitudinal change in the able bodied people. This can happen only through the right education starting at the school level. It needs to be made part of the curriculum so that children can realize how to behave and respond to those with special needs. Moreover, even for adults, there needs to be some courses where these behavioural patterns are instilled. The typical attitude of sympathy is not what is being talked about. It is all about how to treat such people with respect without taking pity on them. They need to be given their space while interacting with them. Moreover, each case of a special disability is unique and one needs to be prepared to respond in an appropriate manner.

One of the chicken and egg quandaries is whether we can create infrastructure in work places when the work force itself has no specially abled people or those who are there don't need the specific facilities being created. In my opinion, it is important for creating the infrastructure so as to enable specially abled people to have the comfort level in applying for openings and entering its precincts. For new buildings, the process is much easier since one can create the requisite facilities from scratch and the costs may not be significant when one considers the overall cost of the building

Moreover, the office spaces need to be ergonomically designed for the specially abled people. One of the key challenges is the spectrum of disabilities and the variations in the severity. There is no *"one size fit all"* solution to how one designs an office.

Public transport in the country needs to be revamped to suit the needs of the people with disabilities. There are a number of features that are well known such as low floor buses, adequate space for having wheelchairs, pre-recorded announcements of bus stops. In the case of the railways, it is important to have proper access to the railway stations all around the country with the use of escalators. A strict enforcement is required to prevent encroachment of the seats and pathways. Specified seats of the coaches near the bathrooms must be kept exclusively for the disabled and the bathrooms must be fitted with the disabled friendly toilets.

In terms of pedestrian walkways, street pavements, recreational areas, overpasses and underpasses it is important to have accessibility for the disabled. This can be in the form of guide strips, tactile markings, curbs, curb ramps and guards should be used to facilitate movement of persons with disabilities. The use of texturized rubber tactile adhesive tiles can provide a strong grip and prevent slipping.

However for public transport and outdoor commute to succeed, the most crucial aspect is the attitudinal change in the people to show the right approach, willing to help but not being too intrusive or condescending.

The medical system should also be geared up to the challenges ahead especially in terms of diagnosis and treatment. The system is burdened with dealing with normal cases and the pandemic also exposed the chinks. It would require a good quantum of funding from the government to set up the state of the art research institutes and treatment centres for such cases.

One of the areas that could be explored is the development of a domestic production base for assistive devices and other products associated with PwD. A production linked incentive (PLI) type scheme could be envisaged for this which would ensure domestic entities taking interest. It would be a win-win situation if these entities can actually employ PwDs in their workforce.

Finally and the most important is the need for skilling of these specially abled people. As stated earlier, they need to be viewed as assets contributing to the economic growth of the country. Such a progressive approach is essential to ensure the building up of confidence among the specially abled and opening up of avenues across various streams for them to find vocational opportunities. With many corporates already embarking on this approach and finding success in it, there is the need for most including the MSMEs to explore this option, even if on a smaller scale.

CHAPTER EIGHTEEN

Conclusions

It is pertinent to note that the government of India has formulated a number of schemes for persons with disabilities but as in any facet of life, the implementation mechanisms are the barometer of success. Therefore, it is imperative that the focus should be on how these can be made facilitative for the specially abled persons who are immobile and are prone to have a low self-esteem, a result of how society has treated them. Moreover, the guardians, already beset with additional responsibilities are in no frame of mind to undertake the plethora of compliances and running around to be done for getting approvals. Therefore one needs to make it facilitative, yet have adequate checks to ensure that only the genuine cases get it.

Moreover, one also has to look at beyond these government schemes. There is a need to take up collective responsibility for ensuring that the specially abled people contribute in their professions. All the stakeholders, including corporates would need to co-ordinate for ensuring better results. The skilling of these persons would be a mutually beneficial outcome namely the financial independence of the employee and their contribution to the economic growth of the country.

In the light of the existing mechanism and looking at some of the international best practices, the key aspects to be kept in mind are the following:

- There are a lot of governmental agencies administering schemes and framing policies for people with disabilities (PwD). One could look at having a more unified structure at the central government level which would ensure effective implementation. The role of State Governments is critical and they must be made partners in this entire effort.

- One of the key aspects is the detection and effective management of the cases at an early stage. For this the medical system has to rise to the occasion. There is a need for setting up of specialized institutions dealing with all types of disabilities. Government funding has to be focused on treatment and research. With the talent pool of medical professionals available, the policy makers would need to think through this.

- Educational system has to be geared to meet these challenges. While standalone schools have their own advantages in being focused, the crucial aspect is to mainstream specially abled children into the education curriculum. Schools should be given the necessary mandate to take in people with all form of disabilities and the government could chip in with technical or human resources. The concept of home schooling is also important for such children depending on their condition.

- Attitudinal change in the able bodied people which can only be inculcated through proper training. Regular courses can be begun at the school level stage to inculcate this behaviour. One could explore refresher courses for others before making them interact with specially abled persons. This would set the tone for ensuring an empathetic attitude and better co-ordination.

-

Use of assistive devices including digital tools and online applications to minimise the interventions are needed for ensuring the effective functioning of these persons. Regular outreaches are needed to disseminate information about the latest technologies. This is also an opportunity for the government to frame a domestic manufacturing eco-system, like the Make in India, on these products by framing a production linked incentive (PLI) scheme for such devices. The employment of PwDs in these entities would be the icing on the cake

- Office spaces to be made more disabled friendly and while this needs to be made mandatory in government run institutions, we must have appropriate incentives for the private sector to adopt such measures. This is essential to ensure that more specially abled people are incentivized to apply.

- Government offices must be asked to undertake necessary audits for compliance with the norms on specially abled on a regular basis. Moreover, all new buildings must have the basic infrastructure which facilitates access with adequate number of assistive devices.

- Accessibility in public transport for the specially abled is crucial and one must focus on the bus and the train system. There are many learnings from the metro system which can be embraced. Some of the features that have been mentioned in earlier chapters include low floor buses, tactile flooring, special seats closer to exit, disabled friendly toilets etc.

- Opening of large scale skilling centres across the country with a focus on the specially abled. Some incentives could be explored for providing resources to the private sector to set up such skilling centres. The industrial parks could also explore this idea through their associations. The private sector should also have adequate incentives for setting up such skilling centres.

- After absorption of the specially abled into suitable vocations, the task does not end there. It is imperative to provide them regular training and ensure a reasonable career path. In the initial phase of their career, they could have a mentor attached to them who can guide them.

- Corporate social responsibility (CSR) is an important pool of funds to be tapped into for ensuring inclusivity. While many corporates are undertaking activities, there is much more needed to be done. The government could provide an incentive by instituting awards for those corporates undertaking exemplary activity under the CSR in this field. This would create a healthy competition and ensure adequate work in this field.

Finally, while one must commend the government in coming out with a number of schemes and framing of policies for specially abled people, there is a still a lot to be done. However, this requires greater participation of all stakeholders. As Robert Hansel said *"When everyone says you can't, determination says, yes you can"*. The specially abled are a determined set of people facing the challenges thrown at them. All we need is to give them is a hindrance free path.
